First published in 2010 in Great Britain by
Barrington Stoke Ltd
18 Walker St, Edinburgh, EH3 7LP

www.barringtonstoke.co.uk

ISBN: 978-1-84299-752-9

Printed in Great Britain by Bell & Bain Ltd

A Note from the Author

I'm not really a big boxing fan. But I am a big fan of Amir Khan.

He's an amazing fighter. You don't become a World Champion at the age of 23 unless you are very good. But he's also an amazing young man. He knows how to make the most of himself. And not just with his fists. Amir Khan knows how to walk the walk. And how to talk the talk.

While I was writing this book I was also writing a book about the racing driver Lewis Hamilton. They are both stories about ordinary kids who have done extraordinary things. And they are both stories about hard work and sticking to one's dream.

Amir Khan is a good role model for young British Asian kids. But everyone can share the story of the boy from Bolton who fought his way to the top.

For Harry

Contents

Chapter 1

Front Row Seat

Athens, 2004. The Olympic Games. The greatest athletes in the world are ready to compete for the medals. Some of them are famous. Some hope to become famous.

The British team hope to do really well in Athens. Everyone expects big stars like Paula Radcliffe and Kelly Holmes to win medals.

But no one thinks Great Britain is going to win a medal for boxing. After all, there is only one boxer in the British Olympic team. And no one has heard of him. He is only 17. He's still at school. He comes from the back streets of Bolton. He is too shy even to talk to the British stars.

What's his name? Amir Khan.

Never heard of him? You soon will.

Chapter 2

A Born Fighter

Amir Khan was born in Bolton on the 8th of December 1986.

His surname means "prince" or "ruler" in Arabic. His family comes from a long line of soldier kings.

Amir's grandfather came to England from Pakistan in 1963. At first he couldn't speak any English. He got a job in Bradford on a potato farm. Then he moved to Bolton to work in a cotton mill.

Amir grew up in a street house in Bolton with his mum and dad, his gran, his brother Haroon, and his sisters Tabinda and Mariyah. His dad ran a scrap-yard in the town. His uncle was a local policeman. His cousin Sajid plays cricket for Lancashire and England.

Amir Khan's family is very important to him. They are very close. They watch all his fights. They all support Bolton Wanderers.

When Amir was small he was a bit of a handful. He had too much energy. He couldn't sit still. He wasn't afraid of anything. When he was only five he climbed up a drain-pipe onto the roof of his house.

Amir went to local primary schools. But he was always in trouble. The teachers didn't know what to do with him. He was always fighting. His mum and dad were worried about him. His gran used to help at the school so she could see what he was up to. But it didn't make any difference. Little Amir was a big problem.

Then one day, when Amir was eight, his dad had an idea. He took his son to a local boxing gym. Amir had never seen anything like it. He loved it. A place where you were allowed to fight! "It was," he said, "totally mad!"

He started training at the gym twice a week. He learned to skip and spar. He

learned to box. He learned karate. But he loved boxing best. He was a natural.

Amir soon started to learn about boxing and about famous boxers. His heroes were the black US boxer Mohammad Ali and the British boxer 'Prince' Naseem Hamed.

He was the smallest boy in the gym, so he had to fight bigger, older boys. But he usually won. His dad said he was "a born fighter".

Now Amir was allowed to fight in the gym, he didn't get into any more fights at school.

Chapter 3

Round 1

Amir's first fight was in December 1997, in Stoke. He was only 11. The other boy was much bigger. But Amir didn't mind. He lasted all three rounds to win on points.

After this he lost a few fights against bigger boys. So he moved to a gym in Bury.

The trainer there was called Mick Jelly. Amir trained hard. He lost some weight. He listened to Mick Jelly's advice. And he won his next 17 fights.

In 2000 he lost in the final of the ABA (Amateur Boxing Association) Junior Championship. The next year he was in the final again. This time he won.

Between January 2001 and February 2004, Amir Khan won 44 fights and lost none.

People soon started talking about the boy boxer from Bolton.

In six months he won the National Schoolboys title, the National Boys Club title and the Junior ABA title. He was picked to fight for England against Scotland and Ireland.

At this time, Amir still had to go to school. He went to a secondary school in Bolton. There he played football, basketball and cricket. He was captain of the school

athletics team. He was the Bolton schools'
champion at 1500m and javelin.

He was the hardest lad in the school. But
he was never in trouble. He was never in
any fights. Everyone respected Amir Khan.

He worked hard at school and passed 6
GCSE exams. He went to Bolton Community
College to study for a BTEC in sports and
fitness. He wanted to study Sports Science at
uni.

But first he wanted to compete in the 2004 Olympic Games in Athens.

Chapter 4

Pulling Up Trees

The ABA are in charge of amateur boxing in Britain. They choose the boxers who will represent Great Britain in the Olympic Games.

The ABA said that Amir was too young to fight in the Olympics. They were worried he would get hurt. They said that the Olympics were for grown men, and Amir was still at school. He hadn't even started to shave.

The ABA let him fight in the Junior Olympics in the USA. Just to see how good he was. He won all his fights and took the gold medal. He even beat the US number one. No British boxer had ever done this before.

They said he could fight in the European Cadet Championship (for under-16s). Just to see how good he was. He won all his fights.

But the ABA were still not sure he was ready for the Olympics. The Americans said he could fight for them if he became a US citizen. But Amir only wanted to fight for Great Britain.

He fought in the European Schoolboys Championships in Italy. He won all his fights and won the gold medal.

In the end the ABA agreed to let him fight in the Olympic qualifiers. If he won, he could compete in Athens.

His first fight was against a big boxer from Georgia. Amir lost on points. But he didn't lose faith in himself. He had four more fights to put things right. And he won them all.

Amir Khan was going to the Olympics!

Chapter 5

Athens

No one gave Amir Khan much of a chance in Athens. Not many people knew just how good he was. But Amir Khan knew. He wanted to win the gold medal.

His first fight was against the Greek number one. The Greek crowd were all on his side, not Amir Khan's. Everyone thought he would win. But Amir Khan stopped him in the 3rd round.

The next fight was against a big boxer from Bulgaria. Again no one thought Amir could win. But he won again.

His 3rd fight was against a boxer from Korea. He was the Asian champion. But Amir Khan knocked him down in the 1st round. The ref stopped the fight.

He swept through the semi-final and won 40-26 on points. Amir Khan was going to be in the Olympic final. Gold or silver – which would it be?

In the final he had to fight Mario Kindelan from Cuba. Kindelan had won gold in the last Olympic games and he was three times World Amateur champion. Amir Khan knew he was fighting the best in the world.

The fight started well. Amir was just ahead on points after the 1st round. But Kindelan won the 2nd round. And the 3rd.

The last round was a draw. It was close, but

Kindelan won 30-22.

Amir Khan was gutted. So were his

family and friends and his army of fans. But

the boy from Bolton had won the Olympic

silver medal.

And he was still only 17 years old.

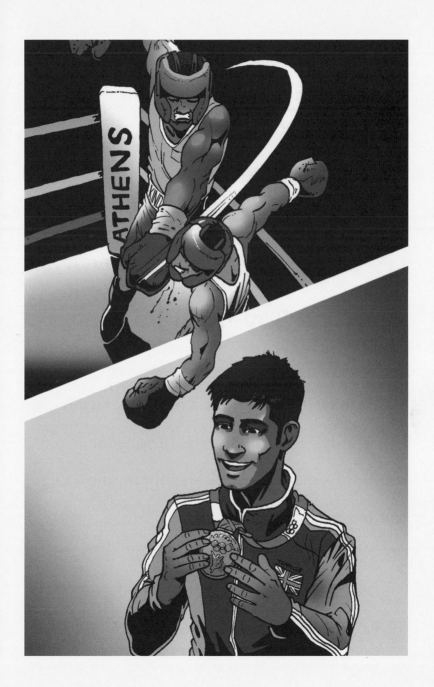

Chapter 6

The Boy from Bolton

Back in Britain, Amir Khan was now a super-star. He was famous. Everyone wanted to meet him. Newspapers and TV wanted to talk to him.

He was a hero in Bolton. He was asked to do a lap of honour, running round the Reebok

Stadium to the cheers of the crowd before Bolton's next home game against Man United. He couldn't believe it.

He met the Queen and the Prime Minister. He was on *Superstars* and *Friday Night with Jonathan Ross*. He was offered record deals and parts in films. "It was totally mad," he says.

He has met lots of famous sports-men and women. He has travelled all over the world.

But he still lives in Bolton. He still
supports Bolton Wanderers. He even trains
at the Reebok Stadium. And his favourite
food is still his mum's curry.

Amir Khan knows he is now a role model.
Most of all for young British Asian lads.

Not long ago Amir spent £1 million of his
own money building a community centre and
boxing gym for kids in Bolton. He says he
wants to show them there are better things
to do with your life than getting into trouble.

Boxing, he says, is all about self-control, hard work and respect.

He does a lot to promote sport and boxing in schools.

He supports the No Messin' programme to stop kids playing near railways.

In 2005 he ran a half-marathon to raise money for people who lost everything when the great Tsunami wave hit the coasts of Asia.

Not long ago he played in a charity football match to raise money for the family of a murdered police-woman.

He raised more than £6,000 for a fire-man who was badly burned while trying to save a family from an arson attack in Bolton.

Every Christmas he visits children in hospital.

After the Kashmir earthquake in 2005, he helped raise lots of money for the survivors.

He went to Pakistan to give out food parcels to children in a refugee camp.

Chapter 7

Pro

After the Olympics, Amir Khan decided to become a pro. This means that he is paid for doing what he does best. Boxing.

He weighs between 59 and 61 kgs. This means he fights as a "Lightweight".

His first fight as a pro was in Bolton in July 2005. It was against David Bailey, who said he was going to knock Amir Khan out. But Bailey found himself on the canvas after only 15 seconds. A minute later the ref stopped the fight.

A few months later, Amir Khan knocked out Mohammed Medjadi after just 55 seconds.

In July 2007 Amir Khan fought Willie Limond for the Commonwealth lightweight title. Limond knocked him down in the 6th round. He seemed to be hurt. But he got

back up and knocked Limond down in the next round. The ref stopped the fight. It was Amir Khan's 13th fight as a pro. He was only 20. But he was already Commonwealth champion.

He defended his title twice that year, first against Scott Lawton and then against Graham Earl. At the time, Earl was the British number one. But after only a minute the ref stopped the fight. Amir Khan had won again. On his 21st birthday.

He defended his title again the following year, winning first against Gairy St Clair, and then against Michael Gomez. Gomez knocked Amir Khan down in the 2nd round. But he got back up and stopped Gomez in the 5th.

In September 2008, Amir Khan lost his first fight as a pro. Breidis Prescott knocked him down after 25 seconds. He got back up, but Prescott knocked him down again. It was the first time he'd lost in 19 fights.

Three months later Amir Khan bounced back, stopping the Irish boxer Oisin Fagan in the 2nd round. Then he would beat world number one, Marco Antonio Barrera.

Since turning pro, Amir Khan has won 19 fights and lost just one. People were starting to ask if he was ready to have a go at the world title.

In July 2009, Amir Khan had his chance at last. He beat Andreas Kotelnik to become World light welterweight champion. The boy from Bolton was the champ! Totally mad!

Chapter 8

Proud to be British

Amir Khan is one of the most famous Muslims in Britain. Islam is very important to him. He prays five times a day and goes to his local mosque on Fridays. He fasts during the month of Ramadan. In 2006 he visited the holy city of Mecca.

He doesn't drink. He doesn't go clubbing.
He doesn't take drugs. He reads the Koran.
He prays in his corner before every fight.

His first pro fight took place only a few
days after the London bombings in July 2005.
The suicide bombers were Muslims. It was a
difficult time to be a young British Muslim.
The fight was at the Bolton Arena. The place
was packed with fans of Amir Khan. It was a
big moment.

When he walked out he was carrying the
Union Jack. The word "London" was stitched

across it. "I wanted to show people that Asian lads like me were proud to be British," he said. His mates in the crowd were waving a huge flag that had both the British and the Pakistani flags on it. Written across the middle were the words, "Knock Out Terrorism".

After the fight, he gave his prize money to the victims of the bomb attacks. "All I could do was stand up and tell the world that not all Asian lads grow up to be mad terrorists and killers."

Amir Khan is proud to be British. He even wears Union Jack shorts. He is also proud to be both a Muslim and a winner.

Chapter 9

For the Record

Amir Khan's house is full of the cups and medals he has won as a boxer. Here are a few:

3 English Schools titles

3 Junior ABA (Amateur Boxing Association) titles

Gold medal, 2003 Junior Olympics

Gold medal, 2004 European Championships

Gold medal, 2004 World Junior Championships

Gold medal, 2004 European Student Championships

Silver medal, 2004 Olympics

At the moment he is:

Commonwealth lightweight champion

WBO Inter-Continental lightweight champion

WBA International lightweight champion

WBA World light welterweight champion

Barrington Stoke would like to thank all its readers for commenting on the manuscript before publication and in particular:

Amas
Callum Clee
Karen Chaffey
Kieran Curwen
Ben Elliot-Holden
Kim Huntington
Craig Mainland
Mattie Margison
Aaron McCrossen
Gail McLeod
Mohammed
Josh Nicholson
Sophie Nicholson
Harry Rose
Danselle Thould
T.J.
Tyler Wood

Become a Consultant!

Would you like to be a consultant? Ask your parent, carer or teacher to contact us at the email address below – we'd love to hear from them! They can also find out more by visiting our website.

schools@barringtonstoke.co.uk
www.barringtonstoke.co.uk

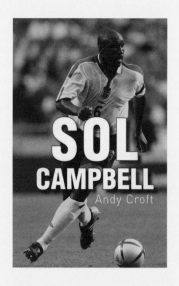

**Kelly Holmes
by
Andy Croft**

From
Defeat
Depression...

To gold medals!
Find out how Kelly Holmes
became an Olympic hero.

**Come On, Danny!
by
Andy Croft**

Danny's dad is in prison.
His teachers are on his
case.
His friends are on his back.
Can he find a way out?

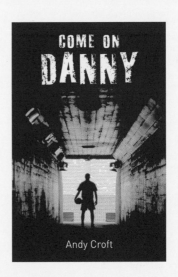

You can order these books directly from our website at
www.barringtonstoke.co.uk